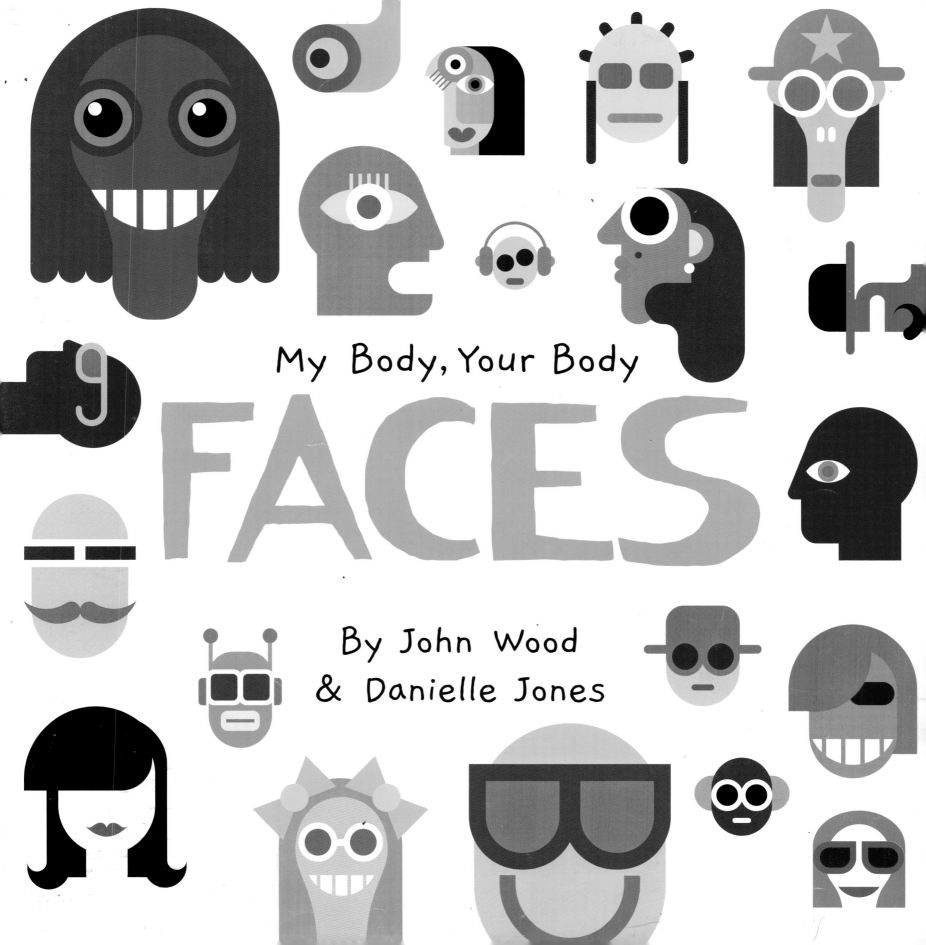

My Body, Your Body

FACES

By John Wood
& Danielle Jones

BookLife
PUBLISHING

©2019
BookLife Publishing Ltd.
King's Lynn, Norfolk PE30 4LS

ISBN: 978-1-78637-740-1

Written by: John Wood

Edited by: Madeline Tyler

Designed by: Danielle Jones

All images are courtesy of danjazzia
via Shutterstock.com, unless otherwise
specified. With thanks to Getty Images,
Thinkstock Photo and iStockphoto.
Additional illustrations by Danielle Jones.

This is my face.

And that
is your
face.

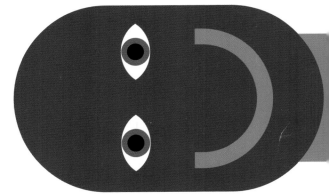

WE ALL
HAVE FACES.

Her face is kind. It is warm.
It is WIDE.

4

His face looks small
when he turns to
one side.

5

His chin is thin.
It is pointy and long.

Her nose is BIG.
It is lovely and strong.

7

This face has dimples

and this face has none.

8

This face is glowing
and round like the Sun.

He starts to **frown** when
he thinks for a while.

10

I can see all of their teeth when they **smile**.

These eyes are brown.
They get **WIDE** when
she speaks.

12

This man has **crinkles**
and lines round his cheeks.

13

Gran has BIG ears,
but she always says

"WHAT?"

14

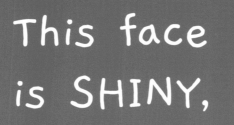

This face
is SHINY,

but this
face is not.

15

Where is this face?

It is covered
with hair!

16

This is a niqab,
which some
people wear.

17

This person has a nice
ring in their nose.

She has **thick** glasses
as red as a rose.

She puts
on make-up.
The colours
are BRIGHT.

20

It takes a **long** time
to get it
just right.

Look at his eyelashes.
They are so long.

Her mouth gets **WIDE** when she sings us a song.

We would go on.
Oh, if only we could!
Faces are **different** and **lovely**
and **good.**

24